Our Class Business

Working at the Same Time

Vanessa Flore

COMPUTER SCIENCE For the REAL World™

Rosen Classroom™

Published in 2018 by The Rosen Publishing Group, Inc.
29 East 21st Street, New York, NY 10010

Book Design: Jennifer Ryder-Talbot
Editor: Caitie McAneney

Photo Credits: Cover, 14 wavebreakmedia/Shutterstock.com; p. 4 Syda Productions/Shutterstock.com; p. 6 (girl) antoniodiaz/Shutterstock.com; p. 6 (rake) StudioOneNine/Shutterstock.com; p. 8 gabriel12/Shutterstock.com; p. 10 Photographee.eu/Shutterstock.com; p. 12 Joyseulay/Shutterstock.com.

ISBN: 9781538352472
6-pack ISBN: 9781508136934

Manufactured in the United States of America

CPSIA Compliance Information: Batch #WS18RC: For Further Information contact Rosen Publishing, New York, New York at 1-800-237-9932

Table of Contents

Learning About Business

Our class has a special guest named Ms. Walker. She started her own business. She created an **app** and now she runs her own business. Ms. Walker wants to teach us how to run a business too.

First, we have to decide what we want our business to be. We look at what's **available** to us. What supplies do we have? What skills do we have?

Goods and Services

Ms. Walker teaches us that businesses sell goods and services. Goods are things you can sell to make money. Services are actions you can do to make money.

We split into two groups to think of ideas at the same time. The first group thinks of goods to sell. They think about selling bracelets, cookies, and school T-shirts. The second group thinks of services. They think about mowing lawns and raking leaves.

Our Materials

What would people buy at school? What is cheap enough to make? We decide to make bracelets.

We have to gather **materials**. Most of the things we need are in our supply closet already. We split into groups to find all we need at the same time. Group One finds beads. Group Two finds string. Group Three finds scissors. We have all the supplies we need to make our bracelets.

Our Assembly Line

We learn about assembly lines. Assembly lines have people and machines working on different tasks at the same time to make a product.

We split into groups again. Group One cuts the string. Each piece of string has to be long enough to wrap around a kid's wrist. Group Two puts the beads onto the string. They use many different colors. Group Three ties the bracelet closed.

Selling Bracelets

Our assembly line worked! We make 100 bracelets in only two hours. We made far more bracelets by working together than we could have made alone.

We sell our bracelets during a school soccer game. Group One tries to get people to buy the bracelets. They wave a sign that says "Bracelets for Sale." Group Two takes people's money when they pay. Group Three counts the money.

A Successful Business

Our class business was a success. We make 100 dollars. We are going to use that money to pay for new books for our classroom.

We learned a lot about business. Ms. Walker says, "Time is money." We can make more money by getting work done in a short amount of time. By working together at the same time, we saved a lot of time. We could make even more bracelets to sell next time!

Glossary

app: A computer program that does a certain task.

available: Able to be used.

material: Something from which something else can be made.

Index